Words Their Way

CLASSROOM

SAVVAS
LEARNING COMPANY

ISBN 13: 978-1-4284-4193-4
ISBN-10:   1-4284-4193-X

11   22

Contents

Suffixes -ment, -less, -ness

-ment	-less	-ness
payment	**worthless**	**darkness**
agreement	useless	politeness
replacement	restless	emptiness
employment	priceless	fondness
government	breathless	kindness
punishment	speechless	neatness
	tireless	friendliness
	flawless	

1. Read each sentence. Choose one word from the box that best completes the sentence. (Note: Not all words have to be used and each word can be used only once.)

2. Add the suffix -ness, -ment, -less, or a combination of these suffixes to the word and write it on the line. (Change -y to i as necessary.)

pay	worth	breath	replace	flaw	speech	empty
use	friendly	punish	dark	fond	kind	neat
agree	price	rest	tire	employ	polite	govern

1. The stitching on the designer gown was _flawless_.

2. After he dropped the phone it was _useless_.

3. Michael was too _rest less_ to sleep.

4. The fake money was completely _worthless_.

5. Did you find a _replacement_ for your lost coat?

6. We reached an _agreement_ after a long discussion.

7. Without a flashlight it is hard to walk in _darkness_.

8. The dog showed its _friendness_ by wagging its tail.

9. The clerk asked for a _payment_ of ten dollars.

10. A judge will decide the criminal's _punishment_.

11. I became _breathless_ while running to the bus.

12. When I lost my job, I started looking for new _employment_.

Prefixes un-, in-, dis-, mis-

un-	in-	dis-	mis-
uneasy	insincere	dishonest	misspell
unaware	informal	disbelief	misleading
untidy	invisible	disease	misbehave
unfasten	indirect	discourage	mistrust
	inexpensive	disconnect	
		disorder	

1. Read each sentence. Choose one word from the box that best completes the sentence. (Note: Not all words have to be used and each word can be used only once.)

2. Add the prefix un-, in-, dis-, or mis- to the word and write it on the line.

~~leading~~	~~formal~~	~~order~~	known	~~direct~~	tidy	behave	~~aware~~
~~belief~~	ease	~~trust~~	~~connect~~	~~fasten~~	~~visible~~	~~expensive~~	courage

1. The party was _unformal_, so we wore our jeans.

2. We didn't take umbrellas because we were _unaware_ it was going to rain.

3. If you pull out the plug, it will _disconnet_ the television.

4. Getting an A on my test was surprising, so I stared at it in _disbelief_.

5. The ad is _Misleading_ because it makes you think you will run fast if you buy the sneakers.

6. Don't _unfasten_ your seatbelt until the plane lands.

7. The shirt was _inexpensie_, so I had enough money to buy it.

8. We took a map when we went hiking on an _unknown_ trail.

9. Don't let losing the game _discorage_ you from playing again.

10. After the party, the room was in _disorder_.

11. My mom promised my sister a reward if she didn't _misbehave_ at the show.

12. The snake is _Invisible_ because it is hidden in the tree.

-ful	-ous	-ious
cheerful	**dangerous**	**envious**
wonderful	marvelous	furious
wasteful	courageous	rebellious
successful	vigorous	studious
delightful	humorous	nervous
	poisonous	
	mountainous	
	outrageous	

...mplete each sentence by adding the ending -ful, -ous, or -ious to the word in parentheses and writing the word on the line. (Make spelling changes, such as dropping -e or -y, as necessary.)

1. A rattlesnake's bite is ___Poisonous___. (poison)

2. We had a ___delightful___ visit with our cousins. (delight)

3. The ___humorious___ story made me laugh. (humor)

4. I was ___Successful___ in finding my lost book. (success)

5. Many bears live in ___mountainous___ areas. (mountain)

6. A ___vigorious___ walk is good for your health. (vigor)

7. My brother was ___furious___ when I arrived an hour late. (fury)

8. Turn off the lights when you go out, so you won't be ___Wasteful___. (waste)

9. The ___rebelous___ teenager did not follow the rules. (rebel)

10. The song lyrics were ___Outrageous___ and shocked everyone. (outrage)

11. Thunder and lightning make my dog ___nerveous___ and scared. (nerve)

12. The party was fun and we had a ___wonderful___ time. (wonder)

Sort 3: Adjective Suffixes -ful, -ous, -ious

Suffixes -ary, -ery, -ory

-ary	-ery	-ory	Oddball
imaginary	**bravery**	**category**	
February	stationery	dormitory	century
ordinary	delivery	directory	
secretary	scenery	victory	
necessary	mystery	inventory	
stationary	machinery	factory	
		history	

1. Read each sentence.
2. Choose one word from the box that best completes the sentence and write it on the line. (Note: Not all words have to be used and each word can be used only once.)

~~machinery~~	dormitory	secretary	mystery	~~ordinary~~	directory
stationery	~~necessary~~	scenery	~~February~~	~~century~~	~~history~~
imaginary	~~factory~~	~~stationary~~	inventory	~~victory~~	~~delivery~~

1. It will be __necessary__ to fix the flat tire before you can ride the bicycle.

2. There is no mail __delivery__ on Sundays.

3. Our team was glad to get a __victory__ after a very long game.

4. We keep small __machinery__, like our snow blower, in the garage.

5. The shortest month of the year is __February__.

6. She wrote thank-you notes on __stationnary__ with her name on it.

7. My favorite subject is __history__, because I like to learn about the past.

8. We toured the ice cream __factory__ and learned how ice cream is made.

9. A __century__ is a period of one hundred years.

10. After taking an __inventory__ of goods in the store, the manager knew what to order.

11. All the cars were __stationery__ until the red light turned green.

12. A dragon is an __ordinary__ creature.

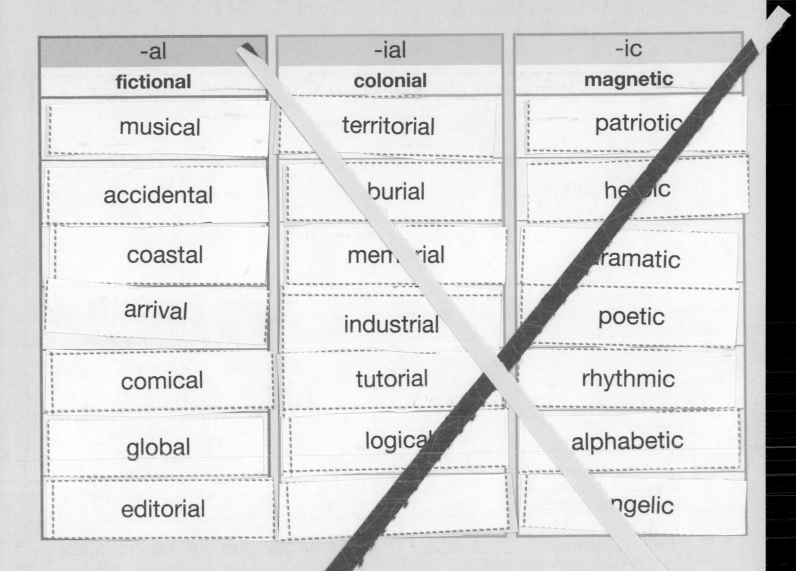

-al	-ial	-ic
fictional	**colonial**	**magnetic**
musical	territorial	patriotic
accidental	burial	heroic
coastal	memorial	dramatic
arrival	industrial	poetic
comical	tutorial	rhythmic
global	logical	alphabetic
editorial		angelic

1. Read each sentence.
2. Choose one word from the box that best completes the sentence and write it on the line. (Note: Not all words have to be used and each word can be used only once.)

coastal	memorial	logical	accidental	arrival
territorial	comical	tutorial	dramatic	heroic
editorial	poetic	patriotic	musical	rhythmic

1. Flying the American flag is a _____patriotic_____ thing to do.

2. The _____coastal_____ storm caused a lot of damage on the beach.

3. An online _____tutorial_____ explained how to put together the bookshelves.

4. The movie was _____comical_____ and made everyone laugh.

5. My favorite singer starred in a _____musical_____ on television.

6. Many people attended the _____memorial_____ service to honor those who died in the fire.

7. The newspaper _____editorial_____ criticized the decision to build a new bridge.

8. The _____rhythmic_____ ticking of the clock helped me fall asleep.

9. I didn't mean to break the glass; it was _____accidental_____.

10. The movie tells the _____dramatic_____ story of people who survive a plane crash.

11. After a long winter, we look forward to the _____arrival_____ of spring.

12. The firefighter's rescue of the boy was brave and _____heroic_____.

Sort 5: Suffixes -al, -ial, -ic

Base -ct	-ct + -ion	Base -ss	-ss + ion
correct	correction	confess	confession
express	possess	instruction	impress
possession	depress	elect	process
discuss	election	discussion	select
expression	collect	impression	procession
selection	subtraction	subtract	protection
collection	instruct	depression	protect

Sort 6: Adding -ion to Base Words, No Spelling Change

(21)

Adding -ion to Base Words, No Spelling Change

Base -ct	-ct + -ion	Base -ss	-ss + -ion
correct	correction	confess	confession

Read each sentence. Choose one word from the pair in parentheses that best completes the sentence and write it on the line. Place an n above the nouns and a v above the verbs.

1. We are reviewing _____ in math this week. (subtract/subtraction)

2. That rare baseball card is my _____. (possess/possession)

3. The fifth graders will vote to _____ a new class president. (elect/election)

4. I have 150 marbles in my _____. (collect/collection)

5. A mother bear will always try to _____ her cubs. (protect/protection)

6. At the end of the day, the bank tellers _____ the checks. (process/procession)

7. We had a _____ about ways to help people in our community. (discuss/discussion)

8. With so many delicious foods, it's hard to _____ my favorite! (select/selection)

9. The _____ on his face was one of pure joy. (express/expression)

10. This summer my father will _____ the swim team at our town pool. (instruct/instruction)

11. The seashell left a perfect _____ in the sand. (impress/impression)

12. Our teacher asked the class to _____ who left the gift on her desk. (confess/confession)

Sort 6: Adding -ion to Base Words, No Spelling Change

Adding -ion and -ian (With No Spelling Change)

Base -t	-t + -ion	Base -ic	-ic + -ian
interrupt	interruption	music	musician
digestion	prevent	magician	electric
exhaust	invention	optician	suggestion
clinic	digest	adoption	clinician
magic	invent	optic	suggest
exhaustion	electrician	adopt	prevention

Adding -ion and -ian (With No Spelling Change)

Base -t	-t + -ion	Base -ic	-ic + -ian
interrupt	interruption	music	musician

Sort 7: Adding -ion and -ian (With No Spelling Change)

1. Read each sentence.
2. Complete each sentence by adding the ending -ion or -ian to the word in parentheses and writing the word on the line. Before adding the ending, think about if the word refers to a person who does something.

1. When the power went out we had to call an _____.
   (electric)

2. She practiced her violin every day to become a better
   _____. (music)

3. The _____ studied only certain diseases. (clinic)

4. Pardon the _____, but I need an answer now. (interrupt)

5. The _____ entertained the children at the party.
   (magic)

6. The scientist's new _____ was a robot that can clean
   floors. (invent)

7. Sitting still can help the _____ of whatever you just
   ate. (digest)

8. My _____ checks my eyesight twice a year. (optic)

9. We liked her _____ so much that we followed it
   immediately. (suggest)

10. We had to put my cat's kittens up for _____. (adopt)

11. After the race, all the runners showed their _____.
    (exhaust)

12. As part of fire _____ week, we practiced exiting the
    school quickly. (prevent)

Sort 7: Adding -ion and -ian (With No Spelling Change)

reproduce	creation	calculate
introduction	hibernation	fascinate
coordination	reduction	concentration
generation	decorate	reproduction
imitation	coordinate	reduce
imitate	concentrate	create
calculation	generate	hibernate
decoration	fascination	introduce

Adding -ion (With e-Drop and Spelling Change)

e-Drop + -tion production	Base -ce produce	e-Drop + -ion location	Base -te locate

Make new words by adding -ion to the following base words. (Drop e and make
spelling changes as necessary.) Then write a definition of the new word.

1. create _____ Definition: _____

2. introduce _____ Definition: _____

3. coordinate _____ Definition: _____

4. reduce _____ Definition: _____

5. fascinate _____ Definition: _____

6. decorate _____ Definition: _____

7. imitate _____ Definition: _____

8. generate _____ Definition: _____

9. reproduce _____ Definition: _____

10. hibernate _____ Definition: _____

11. concentrate _____ Definition: _____

12. calculate _____ Definition: _____

Sort 8: Adding -ion (With e-Drop and Spelling Change)

moist	limb	bombard	haste
muscle	crumb	resignation	limber
columnist	column	soften	designate
hasten	soft	crumble	resign
bomb	moisten	design	muscular

Silent Consonant	Sounded Consonant
sign	**signal**

1. Read the words in the box.

2. Write each word in the column that shows whether it has a silent or sounded consonant.

3. Underline the consonants that alternate between silent and sounded.

bomb	moist	crumb	design	muscle
resignation	designate	muscular	limb	moisten
crumble	limber	hasten	haste	soften
bombard	columnist	soft	column	resign

Silent Consonant	Sounded Consonant

Vowel Alternation: Long to Short

breath	revise	athlete	mine
natural	criminal	revision	breathe
athletic	mineral	crime	nation
nature	national	ignite	grateful
ignition	gratitude	precision	precise

Long Vowel	Short Vowel
type	**typical**

1. Read each sentence.
2. Choose one word from the pair in parentheses that best completes the sentence and write it on the line.
3. Place a long vowel symbol (‾) over the long vowels. Place a short vowel symbol (˘) over the short vowels.

---

1. Esteban had few errors to _____ on his written report. (revise/revision)

2. High in the mountains it is harder to _____. (breath/breathe)

3. Taylor is so _____ that she can run a mile in 6 minutes. (athlete/athletic)

4. Andy showed his _____ for the present by writing a thank-you note. (grateful/gratitude)

5. I left _____ directions so Sue would know where to find us. (precise/precision)

6. They dig up gold and silver in this _____. (mine/mineral)

7. Turning the key in the _____ will start the car. (ignite/ignition)

8. Breaking into someone's house is a _____. (crime/criminal)

9. The company delivers its product to people all across the _____. (nation/national)

10. The _____ home for a bear is the woods. (nature/natural)

Sort 11

Vowel Alternation: Long to Short or /ə/

Base Word Long Vowel	Derived Word Short Vowel	Base Word Long Vowel	Derived Word /ə/
reptile	reptilian	compose	composition
compete	rite	cavity	relative
serenity	define	definition	volcanic
flame	flammable	competition	reside
confide	confidence	cave	volcano
serene	relate	ritual	residence
major	majority		

Sort 11: Vowel Alternation: Long to Short or /ə/ (41)

Vowel Alternation: Long to Short or /ə/

Derived Word /ə/	Base Word Long Vowel	Derived Word Short Vowel	Base Word Long Vowel
composition	compose	reptilian	reptile

1. Read each sentence.
2. Choose one word from the box that best completes the sentence and write it on the line. (Note: Not all words have to be used and each word can be used only once.)
3. Place a short vowel symbol (˘) over the short vowels. Circle the vowels with the schwa sound.

flammable	compose	reptile	definition	compete	composition	relate
volcano	rite	relative	reptilian	confidence	serene	cave
ritual	majority	competition	major	reside	confide	
residence	volcanic	serenity	flame	cavity	define	

1. Can you _____ this word for me?

2. The _____ of marriage is an important ceremony.

3. We were determined to win the _____.

4. The coach showed her _____ in Gabrielle by asking her to lead the warm-up.

5. The _____ of the class attended the baseball playoffs.

6. Do you _____ in this city?

7. The pianist also likes to _____ his own music.

8. The mountain was formed when a _____ erupted.

9. Javier enjoyed the heat of the campfire's _____.

10. The woods were quiet and _____.

11. A snake is a kind of _____.

12. Gasoline is a _____ substance.

inspection	support	portable
perspective	deport	speculate
import	spectator	transport
report	prospect	portfolio
inspector	heliport	spectacle
spectacular	spectrum	opportunity

spect	port
respect	**export**

1. Read the word root in the center of each web and write the meaning below it.

2. Fill in the surrounding ovals with words that contain that word root.

3. Write the meaning below each word.

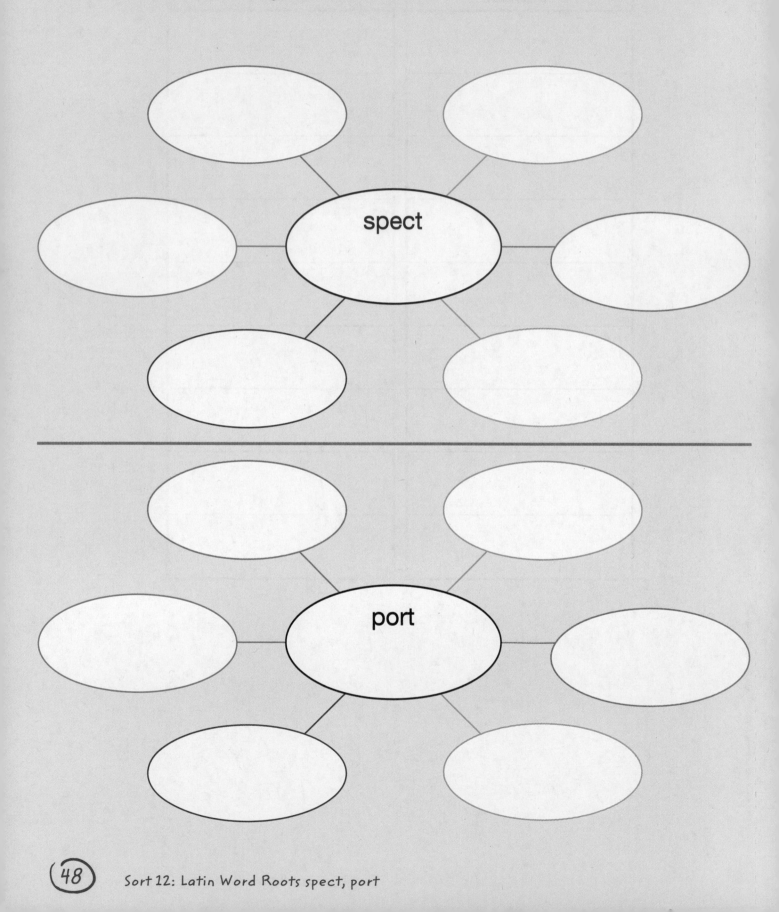

Sort 12: Latin Word Roots spect, port

audible	contradict	auditorium
unpredictable	auditory	verdict
audience	audiotape	dictionary
predict	audition	dictator
audit	diction	audiovisual

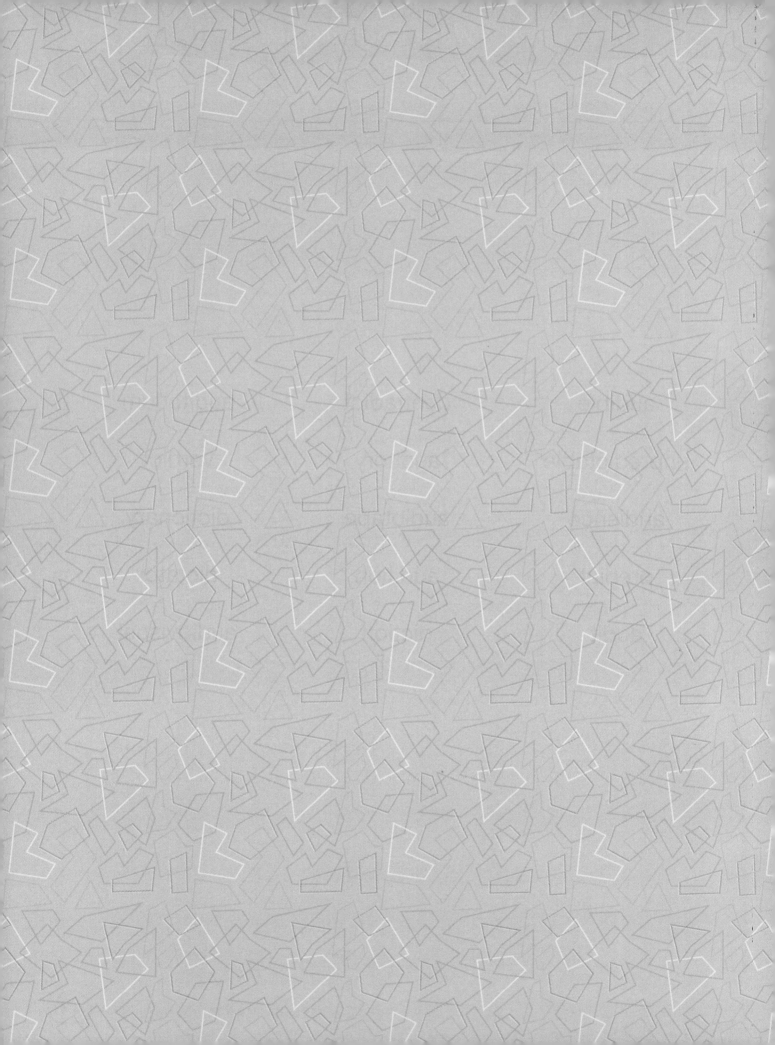

dic	aud
dictate	**audio**

1. Write the meaning of each word root next to the headers.
2. Read each word and circle the word root or roots it contains.
3. Write a definition for each word.

dic: _____   aud: _____

1. diction _____

2. verdict _____

3. auditory _____

4. predict _____

5. audience _____

6. dictator _____

7. audiotape _____

8. contradict _____

9. auditorium _____

10. unpredictable _____

11. audible _____

12. dictionary _____

13. audition _____

14. audit _____

15. dictate _____

Greek Word Parts tele-, phon-, photo-, -graph-

| tele- | phon- | photo- | -graph- |
television	phonics	photograph	graphic
autograph	telegram	calligraphy	headphones
homophone	microphone	phonograph	photographer
telegraph	symphony	telephone	photocopier
telephoto			

Sort 14: Greek Word Parts tele-, phon-, photo-, -graph-

Greek Word Parts tele-, phon-, photo-, -graph-

tele- television	phon- phonics	photo- photograph	-graph- graphic

Sort 14: Greek Word Parts tele-, phon-, photo-, -graph-

55

1. Read the Greek word part in the center of each web and write the meaning below it.

2. Fill in the surrounding ovals with words that contain that word part. (Note: One word will be used in both webs.)

3. Write the meaning below each word.

Sort 14: Greek Word Parts tele-, phon-, photo-, -graph-

general	individuality	neutral	individual
generality	fatality	original	brutal
neutrality	formal	personality	normal
normality	personal	originality	brutality
formality	fatal	mentality	mental
national	inequal	nationality	inequality

Sort 15: Adding the Suffix -ity: Vowel Alternation (/əl/ to Short)

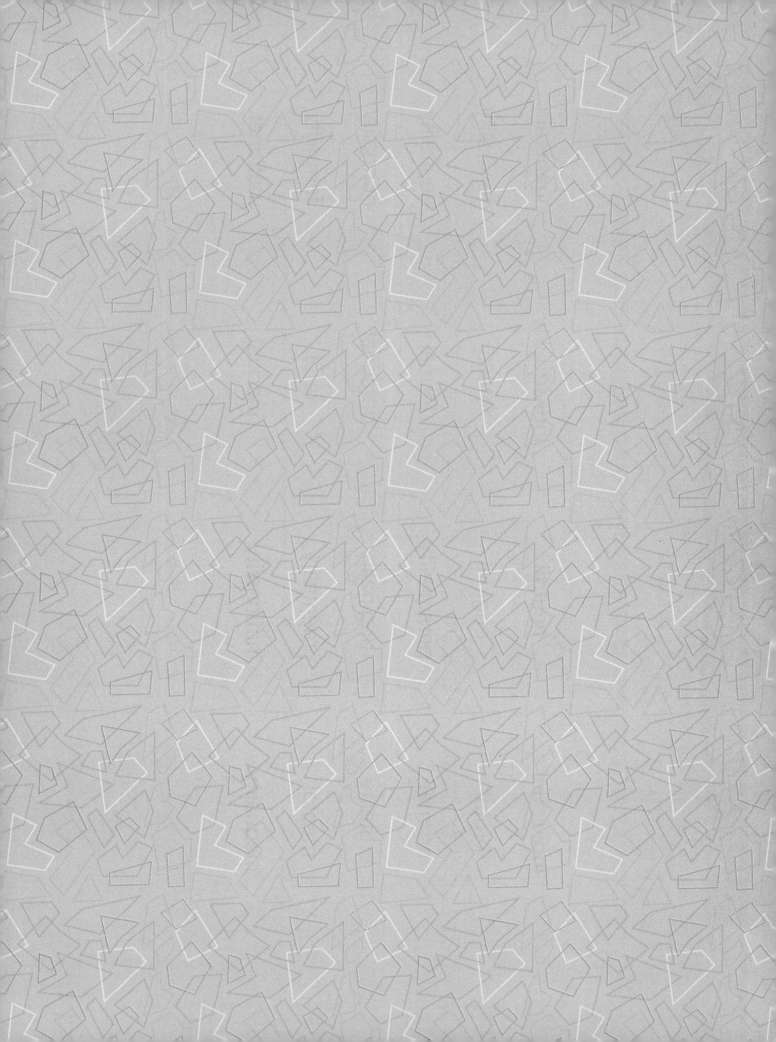

/əl/ moral	-ity morality

1. Read the paragraph below.
2. Find seven words with the sound / əl/ and write them on the lines in the first column.
3. Add the suffix -ity to each word and write the new word on the line next to it.
4. Reread all the words and choose one to use in a sentence.

Jess and Tim went to the general meeting for the art contest. They learned that they had to create original pieces and bring them to the library on National Street in two weeks. They decided to make individual pieces rather than work as a team. Both Jess and Tim created artwork that was very personal to them. Jess used neutral colors and painted one of her best paintings ever. Tim used clay to make an outstanding sculpture. At the formal awards ceremony, both Jess and Tim won prizes for their hard work!

/əl/ Words   **+ -ity**

1. _____   _____

2. _____   _____

3. _____   _____

4. _____   _____

5. _____   _____

6. _____   _____

7. _____   _____

Sentence: _____

_____

_____

Base -m or -n	-ation	Base -e	-ption
exclaim	exclamation	assume	assumption
proclamation	acclaim	acclamation	consumption
presume	explain	presumption	proclaim
consume	resumption	explanation	conception
reclamation	conceive	reception	resume
reclaim	receive		

Base -m or -n	-ation	Base -e	-ption
exclaim	exclamation	assume	assumption

Complete each sentence by adding the suffix -tion to the word in parentheses. (Change the spelling of the base word as necessary.) Write the word on the line.

1. My brother's _____ of vegetables is so large that we have to buy carrots every day. (consume)

2. Paul's _____ of the plan was great, but he did not follow through. (conceive)

3. The king's messenger read a _____ that ended the war. (proclaim)

4. Her _____ helped us understand how to play the game. (explain)

5. The winning team's _____ was heard as soon as the game ended. (exclaim)

6. The _____ of the game began after the rain stopped. (resume)

7. It is a _____ to think you are allowed to enter a home just because a door has been left open. (presume)

8. The _____ of the flooded land began when they pumped out the extra water. (reclaim)

9. Families and school faculty had a _____ to honor students' achievements. (receive)

10. Making an _____ about someone you don't know very well isn't fair. (assume)

64

verification	identification	notification
justification	simplify	simplification
verify	identify	magnify
qualify	notify	justify
clarify	clarification	purify
purification	magnification	unify
qualification	unification	multiply
multiplication		

Base -ify/-iply	Derived -ation
classify	classification

1. Read each sentence.
2. Choose one word from the pair in parentheses that best completes the sentence and write it on the line.
3. Place an n above the nouns and a v above the verbs.

---

1. The campers had to _____ the river water before they could drink it. (purify/purification)

2. We received a _____ in the mail that we were prizewinners. (notify/notification)

3. Amy needed further _____ before she understood what to do next. (clarify/clarification)

4. The family decided to _____ their lives by giving away their television. (simplify/simplification)

5. Can you _____ that this is the correct address? (verify/verification)

6. Malcolm had to show his _____ before he could board the airplane. (identify/identification)

7. The _____ was so strong we could see every hair on the beetle's legs. (magnify/magnification)

8. Rosa had a good excuse to _____ her action. (justify/justification)

9. Akina hoped she would _____ for the track finals. (qualify/qualification)

10. The coach hoped to _____ the team's thinking before the first game. (unify/unification)

Latin Word Roots gress, rupt, tract, mot

gress	rupt	tract	mot
progress	**interrupt**	**attract**	**motion**
subtract	contract	remote	regress
erupt	distract	promotion	attraction
rupture	traction	demote	digress
abrupt	transgress	promote	motivate
disrupt	tractor	emotion	extract
motor	corrupt	interruption	bankrupt

Sort 18: Latin Word Roots gress, rupt, tract, mot

(69)

Latin Word Roots gress, rupt, tract, mot

gress progress							

rupt interrupt							

tract attract							

mot motion							

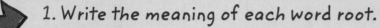

1. Write the meaning of each word root.
2. Read each word and circle the word root it contains.
3. Choose four of the words and write a sentence that uses each word in context.
4. Underline the chosen word in each sentence.

gress: _____ rupt: _____

tract: _____ mot: _____

1. promote   5. subtract   9. erupt
2. distract   6. digress   10. motivate
3. interruption   7. emotion   11. progress
4. disrupt   8. abrupt   12. tractor

Sentences:

1. _____

_____

2. _____

_____

3. _____

_____

4. _____

_____

Sort 18: Latin Word Roots gress, rupt, tract, mot

reject	discredit	injection
eject	objection	manuscript
subject	manage	manufacture
credit	maneuver	credible
projectile	rejection	manicure
manipulate	credentials	

ject	man	cred
inject	**manual**	**incredible**

1. Read each sentence.
2. Choose one word from the box that best completes the sentence and write it on the line. (Note: Not all words have to be used and each word can be used only once.)
3. Circle the word root it contains.

reject	eject	manual	maneuver	discredit	manipulate
projectile	objection	manage	credit	rejection	credentials
injection	manuscript	manufacture	credible	subject	inject

1. The factory was built to _____ canned goods.

2. Ally reached up and caught the _____ .

3. Rita didn't find Tom's story about killer bugs _____ .

4. The doctor hopes a flu _____ will keep the boy healthy.

5. The climber could easily _____ up the mountain.

6. Sam couldn't _____ his store with a broken leg.

7. Maria explained her _____ to the referee's call against her.

8. The pilot had to _____ from the plane when it went out of control.

9. The author spent several years writing the _____ for his novel.

10. My mother asked me to _____ my least favorite paint colors for my room.

11. The _____ of the students' report was plants.

12. We read the _____ before using the computer.

Latin Word Roots scrib/script, fac, struct, vid/vis

scrib/script	fac	struct	vid/vis
scribe	**factory**	**construct**	**visible**
postscript	inscription	facsimile	describe
facilitate	provide	construction	visionary
televise	description	vista	transcribe
improvise	supervise	video	restructure
structure	prescribe	prescription	inscribe
manufacture	vision	visit	transcript

Sort 20: Latin Word Roots scrib/script, fac, struct, vid/vis

Latin Word Roots scrib/script, fac, struct, vid/vis

scrib/script									
scribe									

fac									
factory									

struct									
construct									

vid/vis									
visible									

1. Read each sentence.

2. Choose one word from the pair in parentheses that best completes the sentence and write it on the line.

3. Circle the word root or roots it contains.

1. They _____ car parts in that factory.
   (facilitate, manufacture)

2. I will _____ you with equipment for the rock-climbing trip. (provide/visit)

3. Tara picked up her _____ at the pharmacy.
   (prescription/description)

4. You have to _____ small children very closely.
   (supervise/televise)

5. I will _____ the writing on the cave wall so we can study it later. (inscribe/transcribe)

6. After Aiden signed the letter, he added a _____ at the bottom. (transcript/postscript)

7. Eduardo painted a picture of a _____ of the lake.
   (vista/video)

8. The scientist was such a _____ that he spent all day dreaming of new ideas. (visible/visionary)

9. The class president will _____ the meeting.
   (facilitate, facsimile)

10. The carpenter will _____ a new desk for the office.
    (construction, construct)

11. The doctor can _____ an antibiotic for the infection.
    (prescribe/inscribe)

12. The _____ of the building was very solid.
    (structure, restructure)

Latin Roots duc/duct, ver/vert, fer

Sort 21

duc/duct	ver/vert	fer
introduction	**reverse**	**transfer**
prefer	converse	reduce
deduct	refer	educate
convert	conduct	conductor
vertigo	conversation	defer
conversion		

duc/duct	ver/vert	fer
introduction	**reverse**	**transfer**

1. Read the Latin root in the center of each web and write the meaning below it.

2. Fill in the surrounding ovals with words that contain that root.

3. Write the meaning below each word.

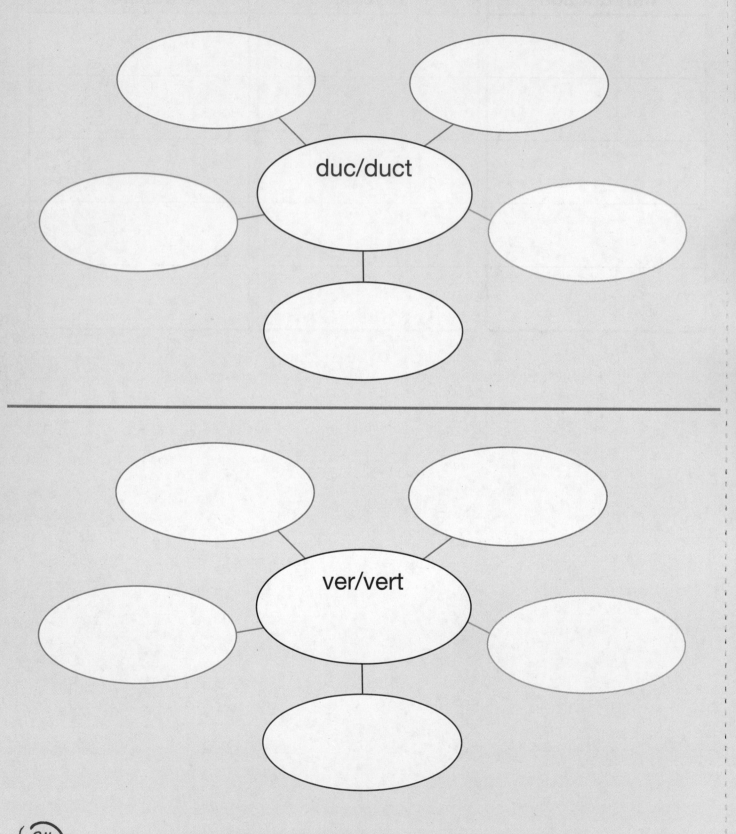

duc/duct

ver/vert

Sort 21: Latin Roots duc/duct, ver/vert, fer

intra-	inter-	intro-	circum-
intrastate	international	introspection	circumference
intravenous	interact	intrapersonal	intracellular
circumscribe	interchange	interpersonal	intercept
introvert	intranational	circumnavigate	Internet
intramural	introversion	intragalactic	interstate

Sort 22: Latin Prefixes intra-, inter-, intro-, circum-

Latin Prefixes intra-, inter-, intro-, circum-

intra- intrastate	inter- international	intro- introspection	circum circumference

Sort 22: Latin Prefixes intra-, inter-, intro-, circum-

(87)

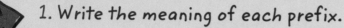

1. Write the meaning of each prefix.
2. Read each word and circle the prefix it contains.
3. Choose four of the words and write a sentence that uses each word in context.
4. Underline the chosen word in each sentence.

intra-: _____   inter-: _____

intro-: _____   circum-: _____

1. Internet	5. intercept	9. intrastate
2. intravenous	6. circumference	10. intracellular
3. intramural	7. international	11. circumscribe
4. interpersonal	8. introvert	12. circumnavigate

Sentences:

1. _____

_____

2. _____

_____

3. _____

_____

4. _____

_____

Adding Suffixes -ent/-ence, -ant/-ance

-ent	-ence	-ant	-ance
different	difference	fragrant	fragrance
abundant	dependent	resident	brilliant
dependence	abundance	brilliance	residence
assistant	dominant	obedience	excellence
confidence	obedient	dominance	patient
prominent	excellent	prominence	distant
distance	relevant	patience	confident
relevance	assistance		

Sort 23: Adding Suffixes -ent/-ence, -ant/-ance

Adding Suffixes -ent/-ence, -ant/-ance

-ent	-ence	-ant	-ance
different	**difference**	**fragrant**	**fragrance**

Sort 23: Adding Suffixes -ent/-ence, -ant/-ance

1. Choose two suffixes (-ent, -ence, -ant, or -ance), and write one in the center of each web. Write the meaning below the suffix.
2. Fill in the surrounding ovals with words that end with the suffix.
3. Write the meaning below each word.

Sort 23: Adding Suffixes -ent/-ence, -ant/-ance

Base + -able	Root + -ible
dependable	**edible**
remarkable	agreeable
adaptable	laughable
plausible	profitable
legible	tangible
preferable	favorable
breakable	predictable
terrible	punishable
decipherable	eligible
feasible	possible
horrible	compatible
gullible	invincible

Base + -able	Root + -ible
dependable	**edible**

1. Read the suffix in the center of each web and write the meaning beneath it.
2. Fill in the surrounding ovals with words that end with that suffix.
3. Write the meaning below each word.

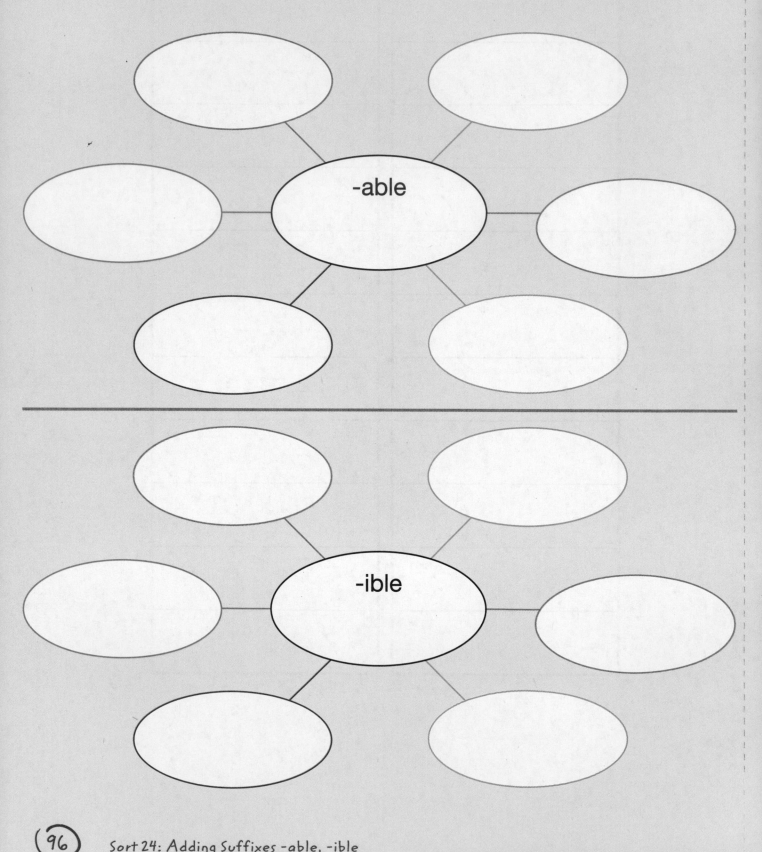

Sort 24: Adding Suffixes -able, -ible

Adding -able and -ible (e-Drop; y to i)

e-Drop + -able	Keep e	Change y to i	e-Drop + -ible
adorable	agreeable	reliable	sensible
defensible	valuable	reusable	manageable
reversible	replaceable	undeniable	identifiable
variable	enforceable	excusable	undesirable
knowledgeable	responsible		

Sort 25: Adding -able and -ible (e-Drop; y to i)

Adding -able and -ible (e-Drop; y to i)

e-Drop + -ible				
sensible				

Change y to i				
reliable				

Keep e				
agreeable				

e-Drop + -able				
adorable				

Read each base word. Add the suffix -able or -ible and write the word on the line. (Drop e or change y to i as necessary.) Then write a sentence that uses the new word in context.

1. excuse _____

2. replace _____

3. vary _____

4. response _____

5. reuse _____

6. manage _____

7. identify _____

8. value _____

9. reverse _____

10. knowledge _____

11. defense _____

12. enforce _____

Prefix Assimilation: in-

in-	im-	il-	ir-
incorrect	**immobile**	**illegible**	**irreplaceable**
inactive	insecure	immortal	incapable
irremovable	immoral	inaccurate	irresponsible
illiterate	inescapable	immigrate	illegitimate
immature	irrational	illegal	irresistible
injustice	illogical	immeasurable	immodest
irregular			

Prefix Assimilation: in-

in- incorrect	im- immobile	il- illegible	ir- irreplaceable

1. **Make new words by adding the prefix in- (in-, im-, il-, or ir-) to the following base words. Write the words on the lines.**

measureable _____	literate _____
justice _____	rational _____
regular _____	migrate _____
legal _____	accurate _____
mortal _____	modest _____
logical _____	legitimate _____
active _____	resistible _____
escapable _____	secure _____
capable _____	mature _____
removable _____	responsible _____

 2. **Choose three of the words and write a sentence that uses each word in context. Underline the chosen word in each sentence.**

1. _____

_____

2. _____

_____

3. _____

_____

Double	Do Not Double
beginner	**canceled**
leveled	forgetting
conferred	limited
quarreling	omitted
preferred	propellant
editing	magnetic
modeling	robotic
forbidden	referred
benefited	orbited

Double	Do Not Double
beginner	**canceled**

1. Read each sentence.
2. Complete each sentence by adding the ending -ed, -ence, -ing, -en, or -ant to the word in parentheses and writing the word on the line. (Double the final consonant of the base word as necessary.)

---

1. The scientist spoke about a new medicine at the _____.
   (confer)

2. I keep _____ to make an appointment with the dentist.
   (forget)

3. Before planting, we _____ the soil to make it even.
   (level)

4. I wanted tacos for lunch, but my friend _____ pizza.
   (prefer)

5. Fuel is a _____ that makes a rocket go. (propel)

6. To raise money for our school, the teachers are _____ clothes at a fashion show. (model)

7. At the end of her report, Ann had made a _____ list to show her sources. (refer)

8. Walking on the train tracks is _____ because it is dangerous. (forbid)

9. I _____ to my notes while giving the speech. (refer)

10. The weather satellite _____ around the earth. (orbit)

11. He spelled the word incorrectly because he _____ the last letter. (omit)

12. When _____ my writing, I often read it out loud. (edit)

Number Prefixes mono-, uni-, bi-, tri-

mono-	uni-	bi-	tri-
monotone	**uniform**	**bilingual**	**triangle**
biceps	triathlon	trigonometry	monopoly
monopod	monolingual	tricentennial	binary
bisect	monologue	bimonthly	bicameral
trilogy	tripod	triennial	monotony
universal	unilateral	biennial	unify
biweekly	monorail	tricolor	triplets

Number Prefixes mono-, uni-, bi-, tri-

mono-	uni-	bi-	tri-
monotone	**uniform**	**bilingual**	**triangle**

Sort 28: Prefixes mono-, uni-, bi-, tri-

(111)

1. Choose two prefixes (mono-, uni-, bi-, or tri-), and write one in the center of each web. Write the meaning below each prefix.
2. Fill in the surrounding ovals with words that begin with that prefix.
3. Write the meaning below each word.

Sort 28: Prefixes mono-, uni-, bi-, tri-

quadr-	quint-	pent-	oct-	cent-
quadruple	**quintuple**	**pentagon**	**octagon**	**centimeter**
octet	percentage	quintuplets	pentangle	quadrant
quadrangle	quadruplets	pentathlon	quintessence	centennial
octave	century	pentathlete	quintessential	quadruped
pentarchy	quadrennial	bicentennial	pentad	

Sort 29: Number Prefixes quadr-, quint-, pent-, oct-, cent-

Number Prefixes quadr-, quint-, pent-, oct-, cent-

quadr-	quint-
quadruple	**quintuple**

pent-	oct-	cent-
pentagon	**octagon**	**centimeter**

1. Write the meaning of each number prefix.
2. Read each word and circle the prefix it contains.
3. Choose four of the words and write a sentence that uses each
   word in context.
4. Underline the chosen word in each sentence.

quadr-: _____   quint-: _____   pent-: _____

oct-: _____   cent-: _____

1. century

2. centennial

3. octagon

4. quadruple

5. quintuplets

6. octave

7. pentagon

8. percentage

9. quadrangle

10. quadruped

11. centimeter

12. quintessential

Sentences:

1. _____

   _____

2. _____

   _____

3. _____

   _____

4. _____

   _____

Sort
30

cap	ped	corp
decapitate	**pedestrian**	**corpse**
corporate	peddle	peddler
pedal	incorporate	capitol
pedicure	corps	corporation
captivity	pedestal	centipede
corporal	captive	captivate
capital	expedition	captain

cap	ped	corp
decapitate	**pedestrian**	**corpse**

1. Write the meaning of each word root.
2. Read each pair of words and circle the word roots in each word.
3. Choose five pairs of words and write a sentence that uses each word pair. For example, The pedestrian packed a backpack and went on a great expedition. (pedestrian/expedition)

cap: _____ **ped:** _____ **corp:** _____

Word Pairs

1. pedicure/peddler

2. corporate/corporal

3. captivate/captive

4. pedal/peddle

5. capital/capitol

6. pedestrian/expedition

7. corps/corpse

8. centipede/pedestal

Sentences:

1. _____

_____

2. _____

_____

3. _____

_____

4. _____

_____

5. _____

_____

onym	gen	mort
antonym	**genesis**	**mortal**
mortician	homonym	pseudonym
progenitor	generator	progeny
patronymic	mortified	genetic
genre	immortal	acronym
regenerate	anonymous	hydrogen
eponym	generic	synonym
gene		

Greek and Latin Word Roots

gen, mort, onym

onym	gen	mort
antonym	**genesis**	**mortal**

1. Choose two word roots (gen, mort, or onym) and write one in the center of each web. Write the meaning below each word root.
2. Fill the surrounding ovals with words that contain that word root.
3. Write the meaning below each word.

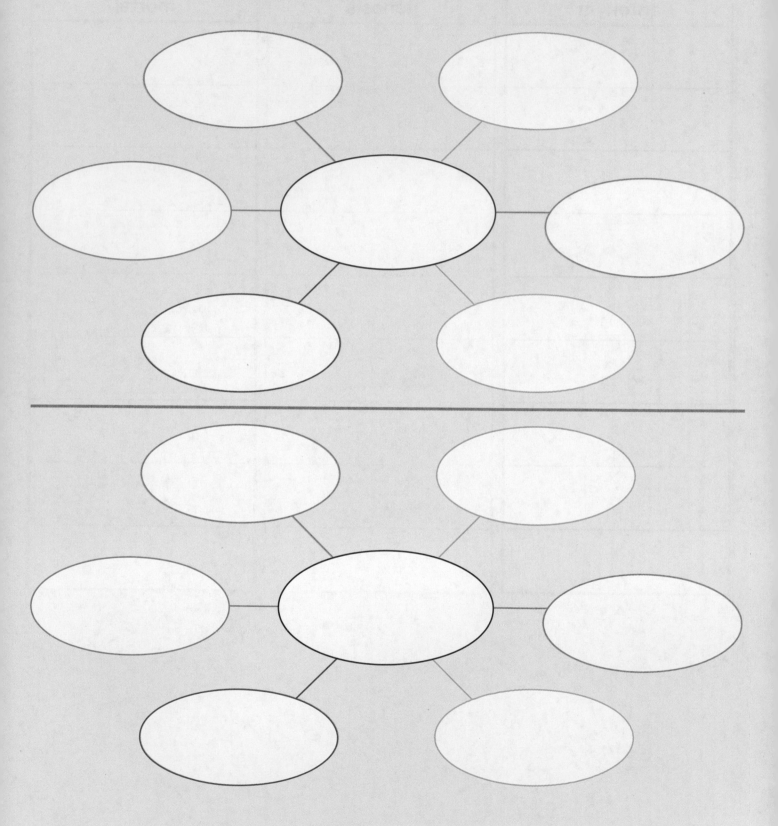

Sort 31: Greek and Latin Word Roots gen, mort, onym

sect	junct	spir
dissect	**junction**	**perspire**
expire	insect	conjunction
section	spiritual	conspiracy
inspiration	respiration	juncture
sectarian	transpire	intersection
conspire		

sect	junct	spir
dissect	**junction**	**perspire**

1. Read each sentence and the word root in parentheses.
2. Complete each sentence by writing a word that contains that word root.
3. Circle the word root in your word.

1. Nature was my _____ to write the poem. (spir)

2. The mosquito is an annoying _____. (sect)

3. The man led a _____ to overthrow the government. (spir)

4. The word <u>and</u> is a commonly used _____. (junct)

5. We will _____ together to plan a surprise party. (spir)

6. There is always a lot of traffic at the busy _____. (sect)

7. Our free movie pass will _____ soon. (spir)

8. She doesn't know what will _____ after her project is done. (spir)

9. For some people, yoga is a _____ practice. (spir)

10. The _____ at the front of the auditorium was reserved for the graduates. (sect)

11. At this _____, it is too soon to know how widespread the illness will be. (junct)

12. After racing, the boy had to rest until his _____ was back to normal. (spir)

Sort 32: Latin Roots sect, junct, spir

jud	leg	flu
judge	**illegal**	**fluent**
flume	legislate	misjudge
legal	judicial	fluency
judgmental	legacy	legislator
fluctuate	privilege	flush
legalize	legitimate	influence
judiciary	prejudge	prejudice
judgment	fluid	influenza

Latin Word Roots jud, leg, flu

jud	leg	flu
judge	**illegal**	**fluent**

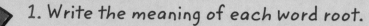

1. Write the meaning of each word root.
2. Read each word and circle the word root it contains.
3. Choose five of the words and write a sentence that uses each word in context.
4. Underline the chosen word in each sentence.

jud: _____ **leg:** _____ **flu:** _____

1. legislate
2. fluctuate
3. illegal
4. judicial

5. influence
6. prejudge
7. influenza
8. legacy

9. judgmental
10. legitimate
11. fluent
12. legislator

Sentences:

1. _____

   _____

2. _____

   _____

3. _____

   _____

4. _____

   _____

5. _____

   _____

Greek and Latin Word Roots voc, ling, mem, psych

voc	ling	mem	psych
vocal	**linguist**	**memory**	**psychology**
vocalic	linguaphile	memorandum	sociolinguist
vocabulary	psychiatry	memorial	immemorial
remembrance	advocate	invocation	psychopathology
linguini	provocative	psycholinguists	provoke
multilingual	commemorate	invoke	provocation

Sort 34: Greek and Latin Word Roots voc, ling, mem, psych

voc	ling	mem	psych
vocal	linguist	memory	psychology

Sort 34: Greek and Latin Word Roots voc, ling, mem, psych

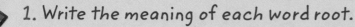

1. Write the meaning of each word root.
2. Read each word and circle the word root it contains.
3. Choose five of the words and write a sentence that uses each word in context.
4. Underline the chosen word in each sentence.

voc: _____   ling: _____   mem: _____   psych: _____

1. provocation
2. linguini
3. commemorate
4. psychiatry

5. memorial
6. linguaphile
7. advocate
8. vocabulary

9. provocative
10. remembrance
11. memorandum
12. sociolinguist

Sentences:

1. _____
   _____

2. _____
   _____

3. _____
   _____

4. _____
   _____

5. _____
   _____

Latin Roots press, pur/purg, fus, pend

press	pur/purg	fus	pend
pressure	**purge**	**transfusion**	**pendulum**
diffuse	impure	infusion	confuse
pendant	impressive	expurgate	impending
Puritan	oppressive	perpendicular	purification
suspend	compression	suspenders	

Latin Roots press, pur/purg, fus, pend

press	pur/purg	fus	pend
pressure	**purge**	**transfusion**	**pendulum**

1. Read each sentence.
2. Choose one word from the box that best completes the sentence and write it on the line. (Note: Not all words have to be used and each word can be used only once.)
3. Circle the word root it contains.

infusion	confuse	pendant	suspend	impressive
impure	impending	Puritan	compression	expurgate
diffuse	oppressive	suspenders	purification	perpendicular

1. A green _____ hung from a chain on Rosa's neck.

2. Sanil wore _____ instead of a belt to hold up his pants.

3. Her high score in the competition was _____.

4. The lawyer prepared for the _____ trial.

5. The heat was so _____ that we stayed indoors in the air conditioning.

6. The editor decided to _____ a chapter before publishing the book.

7. I offered to help Kim _____ some decorations from the ceiling.

8. Our town's _____ plant makes our water safe to drink.

9. It is easy to _____ the twins because they look so much alike.

10. The _____ air makes it difficult to breathe.

11. We opened a window to _____ fresh air throughout the room.

12. Jack's behavior is influenced by strict _____ values.

Latin Roots pas, loc, sist, sta/stat/stit

pos	loc	sist	sta/stat/stit
position	**locate**	**insistent**	**statue**
compose	location	composite	obstacle
consistent	deposit	dislocate	establish
instability	locomotion	persistent	relocate
disposable	substitute	constitution	

Latin Roots pos, loc, sist, sta/stat/stit

pos **position**	loc **locate**	sist **insistent**	sta/stat/stit **statue**

Sort 36: Latin Roots pos, loc, sist, sta/stat/stit

(143)

1. Read each sentence.
2. Choose one word from the box that best completes the sentence and write it on the line. (Note: Not all words have to be used and each word can be used only once.)
3. Circle the word root it contains.

compose	substitute	consistent	relocate	instability
establish	disposable	location	composite	constitution
persistent	dislocate	obstacle	deposit	locomotion

1. When the tree fell in the storm it created an _____ on the road.

2. My baby sister has a _____ naptime.

3. After wearing the _____ gloves, she threw them out.

4. This week, Mr. Mark is the _____ for our teacher who is out sick.

5. When my mom got a new job in a new city, our family had to _____ .

6. She went to the bank to _____ her money.

7. It takes a lot of talent to _____ a piece of music.

8. The owner of the new bakery gave away samples to help _____ his business in the community.

9. The meeting is in a central _____, close to where everyone lives.

10. Jon was _____ in asking for a cell phone for his birthday.

11. Crawling is the baby's form of _____ .

12. The rules of the club are written in its _____ .

ceiv/cep	tain/ten	nounce/nunc
deceive	**retain**	**pronounce**
deception	retention	pronunciation
detain	perception	preconception
preconceive	perceive	attention
detention	attain	sustenance
renounce	denounce	renunciation
denunciation	abstain	sustain
abstention		

ceiv/cep	tain/ten	nounce/nunc
deceive	**retain**	**pronounce**

1. Choose two spelling changes (ceiv/cep, tain/ten, or nounce/nunc), and write one in the center of each web.
2. Fill the surrounding ovals with pairs of words that use the spelling change. For example, retain/retention.

Sort 37: Predictable Spelling Changes ceiv/cep, tain/ten, nounce/nunc

com- **combine**	col- **collaborate**	con- **connection**
ad- **advertise**	ob- **obsolete**	sub- **subtraction**
appetite	companion	appendix
conclude	suppress	oppose
committee	suspect	collateral
congregation	aggressive	collision
attribute	accommodate	offensive
supportable		

com-	col-	con-
combine	**collaborate**	**connection**

ad-	ob-	sub-
advertise	**obsolete**	**subtraction**

1. Read each sentence.
2. Choose one word from the box that best completes the sentence and write it on the line. (Note: Not all words have to be used and each word can be used only once.)
3. Circle the prefix it contains.

conclude	appetite	committee	congregation	accommodate
companion	suppress	suspect	aggressive	supportable
appendix	oppose	collateral	collision	attribute

1. After a day of hiking, I always have a big _____.

2. The _____ met to discuss plans for the film festival.

3. I am leaving early because I _____ there will be a long line for the movie.

4. Her sense of humor is her best _____.

5. The cars were involved in a _____ when the traffic light was broken.

6. Many people _____ building a new bridge because of the high cost.

7. The van can _____ ten passengers.

8. Andy's dog has been a loyal _____ for many years.

9. We will _____ the meeting after everyone has a chance to speak.

10. I tried to _____ a cough in the crowded theater.

11. The bank required the man to put up _____ to ensure he will repay the loan.

12. Our school started an _____ campaign to promote physical fitness.